COLOURFUL AUSTRALIA
PERTH

Produced by
Ted Smart & David Gibbon

Featuring the Photography of
Øystein Klakegg

Published by Colour Library Books for
GORDON & GOTCH LTD

ARAFURA SEA

TIMOR SEA

INDIAN OCEAN

CORAL SEA

TASMAN SEA

Torres Strait

DARWIN

Arnhem Land

GULF OF CARPENTARIA

Cape York Peninsula

Kimberley Plateau

NORTHERN TERRITORY

Barkly Tableland

Cairns

Great Sandy Desert

Cloncurry○ Richmond○

Townsville

○ The Granites

QUEENSLAND

Mackay

Macdonnell Ranges

Rockhampton

Gibson Desert

○ Alice Springs

WESTERN AUSTRALIA

△ Ayers Rock Simpson Desert

Bundaberg

Lake Eyre Basin

Charleville○

Ipswich

Shark Bay

Great Victoria Desert

Lake Eyre

Grey Range

Toowoomba○ BRISBANE

SOUTH AUSTRALIA

GREAT DIVIDING RANGE

GREAT BARRIER REEF

Geraldton○

NEW SOUTH WALES

Nullarbor Plain

○ Kalgoorlie

Flinders Range

Broken Hill○

Maitland○

PERTH
Fremantle○

Port Pirie○

Newcastle

SYDNEY

Elizabeth

Wollongong

Spencer Gulf

ADELAIDE

CANBERRA

VICTORIA

Ballarat○ MELBOURNE

SOUTH AUSTRALIAN BASIN

Geelong○

Bass Strait

TASMANIA

○ Launceston

Queenstown○

Hobart

Published in Australia by Gordon & Gotch Ltd.

First published in Great Britain 1984 by Colour Library Books Ltd.
© 1984 Illustrations and text: Colour Library Books Ltd.,
Guildford, Surrey, England.
Colour separations by Llovet, Barcelona, Spain.
Printed and bound by Gráficas Estella, Spain.
All rights reserved.

ISBN 0 86283 135 0

TITLES IN THE COLOURFUL AUSTRALIA SERIES
Animals of Australia
Wild Flowers of Australia
Perth
Koalas
Melbourne
Tasmania
Adelaide
Brisbane
Canberra
Sydney
Ayers Rock and the Olgas
The Great Barrier Reef
The Outback

State Capital of Western Australia, the sunshine city of Perth enjoys a wonderful climate. Straddling the blue waters of the Swan River – the natural habitat of the black swan – it is situated 19km above the port of Fremantle, which opens into the Indian Ocean. From here arises a sea breeze, 'the Fremantle doctor', which cools the population of 925,000 on hot summer afternoons.

It was in the early nineteenth century that the British, anxious about the intentions of the United States and France, decided to settle on the western coast of Australia and to claim the entire continent as their own. The move was no doubt prompted by recent colonial wars in India and America. These series of wars had their roots in the fact that both Britain and France had established colonies near to each other. The wars had been expensive in lives and money and the British Government was determined that the same situation should not develop in the potentially profitable land of Australia.

Until the 1820s Britain had only claimed the eastern part of the continent and even there the settlements were very small. In 1827, Captain James Stirling sailed along the western coast of Australia, charting the seas and looking for a good site for settlement. He returned with such glowing reports that several capitalist adventurers became interested in founding a colony. Two years later Captain Stirling returned and, on June 17 1829, read out a proclamation declaring that the whole western third of Australia belonged to Britain and that he was to be the first Lieutenant Governor. Though he only had 150 settlers with him, James Stirling was not in the least daunted by the prospect of settling an area ten times the size of Britain. Fremantle was founded at the mouth of the Swan River, to act as a port, and a slight hill was named Perth and declared to be the capital city. Within two years the population had increased tenfold to 1,500 souls, and the town has never looked back.

Today, the settlement has grown into a city bustling with life and reflects well the prosperity of Western Australia. It is in this context that it should be seen, serving 1.3 million people in an area nearly one-third the size of the continent. It is the most isolated capital in the world, with Adelaide 2,700 km to the east, along a road that was not even paved until 1976. This isolation shaped its history and character. Twelve thousand sea miles away from England, the early settlers had to be independent and hardy. They had to fight both the unforgiving land and harassment by Aborigines. Struggling together, the essential spirit of the people was forged true and strong. Elegant Perth was proclaimed a city in 1856 and a lord mayoralty in 1929, but it had a slow rate of growth until a small Irish tramp discovered one of the richest reefs of gold ore in the world. The gold was deep in the interior around the Coolgardie-Kalgoorlie area. From 1890 onwards thousands of hopefuls poured into the state and gold poured out. Perth, as the main port of the state, benefited enormously in wealth and population. Expansion was further aided by the telegraph link to Adelaide in 1877, and the improved Fremantle harbour of 1901. The trans-continental highway was completed in 1917 and today Perth is accessible by several highways, as well as by its international airport.

Although the city is a major industrial centre, the heavy industries are concentrated in Fremantle, Welshpool and Kwinana. Prosperity relies on steel, aluminium and nickel; paint, plaster, cement and rubber, as well as petroleum refineries and food-processing plants. The mineral wealth of Western Australia pours into Perth; there are huge deposits of iron in the state, as well as diamonds, bauxite, uranium and gold. There are also amongst the world's largest deposits of cobalt, vanadium, molybdenum, tantalum and chrome – the so-called strategic metals. The state is not only rich in mineral wealth; agriculture also plays a vital role in the economy. The land around Perth itself is rich and fertile, producing a wide range of crops. Even the drier land in the far north produces its share of wealth in the form of wool and beef.

The excellent climate makes all kinds of outdoor sports popular. Sailing is a passion with some people and those not in boats can surf, swim or laze in the sun on the white, sandy beaches. Other favourite sports include hockey, cricket, bowls and tennis. Winter sports include "Australian Rules" football: a game with machismo. The post-war immigration accounts for the existence of soccer too. For others there is basketball, speedboat and car racing. It is all there for the taking!

Perth has been most fortunate in preserving its natural heritage. John Septimus Roe was the first surveyor general of the colony, and he was responsible for the setting aside of land for the public. He also banned the felling of trees on Mount Eliza. The result of his work is King's Park: a thousand acres of natural bushland overlooking the city and a source of much civic pride. Here is the War Memorial, where you may stand humbled before the obelisk to those who died in distant, foreign lands, so far from the peace and beauty of these sylvan paths. Not too far away there is also Yanchep Park, Queen's Park, Hyde Park and the John Forrest National Park. Just 20km offshore there is the holiday resort of Rottnest Island, home of the quokka. Doctors have discovered that this small marsupial has the ability to regenerate its muscle tissue when injected with massive doses of vitamin E. This may lead towards a cure for muscular dystrophy.

The University of Western Australia is resposible for developing a mechanical sheepshearing machine, which can equal a man's time of three minutes. There is also a technical college, two teachers' training colleges and some private colleges. Perth has both Anglican and Roman Catholic cathedrals, and several historic buildings: the Barracks Arch, His Majesty's Theatre, the Town Hall with its clock tower, the Old Asylum, the Old Mill and Government House dating back to 1863.

Perth is still at the frontier of a vast land, where children learn from the Schools of the Air and medical care is a visit from the flying doctor. Tempered by a history of struggle, the city stands gracefully, embracing a golden people of vibrant energy.

Previous pages a twilight view of the city from Kings Park. *These pages* The Entertainment Centre on Wellington Street *bottom left*, the Commonwealth Government Centre *bottom centre* and the Concert Hall *bottom right* reveal the type of modern architecture that is springing up in Perth. The Parliament House *right*, however, belongs to another era.

Barrack Street *left and facing page* runs along the side of the central shopping mall, as does Murray Street *above* and William Street *below*. The Mall is an area of central Perth where vehicles are prohibited and pedestrians can shop in peace and quiet. The Mall includes a sizeable section of Hay Street where many large stores and small shops line its streets. *Top left* London Court.

The thriving city of Perth has built its prosperity, in part, upon the mineral wealth of the state. This prosperity is increasingly apparent in the modern buildings of the city. The Art Gallery of Western Australia *facing page*, completed in 1979, won a major architectural award when it was built and has since proved to be a magnificent addition to the civic amenities. The AMP building *right* is another noted landmark in Perth, as are the buildings along Saint George's Terrace *below right*. Cinema City is seen *bottom left* reflecting the Town Hall clock. *Overleaf* Perth and its racecourse, which is to be found at Belmont Park.

Previous pages a magnificent view of the city from the AMP building, showing the natural beauty of the city's setting.
Above a gnarled tree stands watch over a park in Fremantle, Perth's port. Many of the important buildings in the city are surrounded by gardens of great beauty. *Far left* and *facing page below* the neo-Gothic Catholic cathedral, which stands amid trees and shrubs in Victoria Square while the gardens *facing page top* lie before the Parliament Buildings. The strange Ore Obelisk *left*, which is to be found in Stirling Gardens, was erected to mark the arrival of the millionth inhabitant of Western Australia.

Previous pages the city of Perth takes on a new image at night. His Majesty's Theatre *below* is a glorious example of a style of architecture little used today, as are the arches on Roe Street *left*. *Centre left* Forrest Place. The Carrillion Centre *facing page* is an impressive example of modern architecture put to practical use as a shopping complex. Opened in March 1983, this four-level centre cost some twenty-six million dollars. A less inspired piece of architecture is the bus station *bottom left*. The view of the city *overleaf* was taken from the south side of the Swan River.

The towering business centre *previous pages* is an indication of the wealth which has come to Perth as a result of the booming population and industry of the area. Among the parks and gardens of Perth, *bottom right* Queens Gardens and *facing page* Kings Park, many historic buildings survive from the colonial era. Turner Cottage *left* and *below* has been restored to its original condition. The Old Mill *below left* was built in the earliest days of Perth, during the 1830s, to grind the flour of the fledgling colony. Today, it is a museum and its grounds contain many interesting relics, including a mail coach and a blacksmith's forge.

Kings Park offers superb views of the city *these pages*. In this park, which was created by the city's founders stands the War Memorial on Anzac Bluff *above left*, a monument to the heroism of Australians in two World Wars. Beyond the memorial can be seen Melville Water, where the Swan River spreads out before it meets the ocean at Rous Head.

Located in the pleasant suburb of Crawley, the University of Western Australia *these pages* is the main seat of learning for the state. Its dignified buildings, *above* and *below* Winthrop Hall, stand amid greenery. *Overleaf* seen from Kings Park, the lights of night-time Perth are spread out like a carpet.

Perth has come a long way from the collection of pioneer buildings erected by Captain Stirling in 1829. Today, the tall buildings of the business heart of the city tower above the shops and houses.

Perth Zoo was first opened in 1898 and at once gained a reputation for excellence that it has retained ever since. Today, it houses a wide variety of Australian wildlife in modern, spacious surroundings; among them are: *above* a wallaby, *far left* kangaroos, *top* pelicans and *facing page* the black swan after which the Swan River was named. *Overleaf* the skyline of modern Perth.

The flora of Western Australia has been shaped by its geological history and its climate. Its original connection with the other southern continents in the supercontinent of Gondwanaland gave Australia its multitude of plant families. The recent change in the continent's climate has had an equally marked effect on the plants. As the atmosphere became drier and hotter, the plants had to adapt to survive. One of the ways in which they did this was to develop small, narrow and waxy leaves that allowed for very little surface evaporation. The plants on *these pages* show this process, known as sclerosis, to perfection. *Left* scarlet honeymyrtle, *above* wiry honeymyrtle, *top right Isopognon lanenthifolia, top left Grevillea* and *facing page* the dramatic bloom of the *Beaufortia*.

Red is a vibrant colour which features strongly among the flowers of the great antipodean continent. The rose coneflower *Isopognon formous facing page* and the red pokers *Hakea bucculenta top right* both belong to the Protaceae family, which is perhaps better known as the Grevillea family. The range of this family in Australia and South Africa is a powerful clue to the previous existence of Gondwanaland, the vast southern continent of dinosaur times, which was later to divide into the continents of Africa, South America, Antarctica and Australia. The Myrtaceae family, to which belong Baxter's kunzea *Kunzea baxteri left* and the delicate murchison clawflower *Calothamnus homalophyllus top left*, is restricted to Australia and a few nearby islands. *Above* the gorgeous shades of the *Diplolaena augustifolia*.

Previous pages show the interchange near Kings Park. *These and following pages* in the spring of 1983 it seemed as if the whole of Perth went mad. People cheered in the streets, pubs stayed open and beer and wine flowed like rivers. For weeks the city had been on tenterhooks, waiting for news of the America's Cup from Rhode Island, USA. Time after time the American judges, who had formulated the rules themselves, put off the races because the wind was too light or too variable. But eventually Alan Bond's yacht *Australia 2* crossed the finish line ahead of its rival and the team brought the America's Cup home to Perth amid almost fevered rejoicing. Pictures by Michael Coyne/Talentbank.

Previous pages the riverside and seaside location of Perth makes watersports popular with its residents. Fremantle was founded in the same year as Perth to act as the capital's seaport; a role it has filled admirably ever since. *These pages* the harbour *top right, top left* and *far left* is kept busy loading ships with the rich minerals that are the chief wealth of the state. The excellence of the Town Hall *left* and of the parks *above* reflect the prosperity that trade has brought. The stalls of Fremantle Market *facing page,* which is housed in a large Victorian building, will sell almost anything.

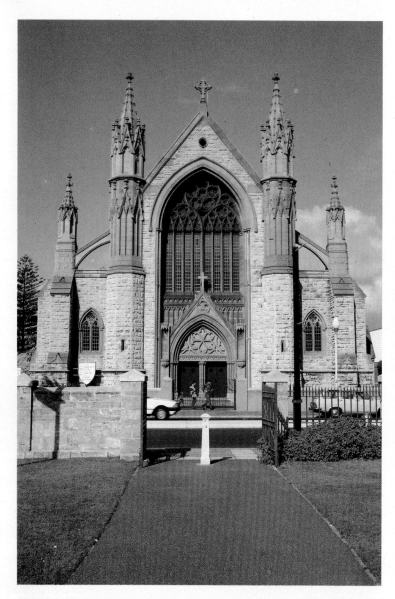

Though Fremantle *these pages* is often overshadowed by its larger neighbour, it has much to offer resident and visitor alike. The Round House Gaol, a grim reminder of days gone by, *facing page, bottom* stands alongside the High Street *facing page, top* and *left*. The magnificent buildings of the Market *far left*, the Harbour *above*, the Museum *top right* and Saint Patrick's Catholic Church *top left* are all based on European architectural styles.

Around Perth can be found many places well worth a visit. Rottnest Island *facing page, top* and *left* is a popular resort, with spectacular scenery and a charming colony of quokkas. Yanchep National Park, on the other hand, is on the mainland a few miles north of the city. It is famous for its magnificent coastal scenery *facing page, below,* abundance of cuddly koalas *above* and spectacular underground caves. In the fertile southwest of the state are many sheep stations, such as that near Jurien *far left.* Sheep ranching is an important aspect of the area, as is market gardening and other types of agriculture. *Overleaf* the atmospheric caves in Yanchep National Park.

The wildlife of the south
west of Western Australia
is typical of the
continent. The black swan
below right, near Jurien,
the grey kangaroo *below* and
the Koala, *top* and *main
picture* at Yanchep, are not
found outside Australia.